Destined to Know God Personally

Marty Delmon
The Destined Series — Book 11

Destined to Know God Personally
By: Marty Delmon

All rights reserved. No part of this book may be reproduced or transmitted in any form or by any means, electronic or mechanical, including photocopying, recording, or by any information storage and retrieval system, without written permission from the author, except for the inclusion of brief quotations in a review. For information, please contact the publisher.

Copyright © Marty Delmon, 2017

Front Cover: Genesis - Bible - Creation - Father & Son
© Carlo Toffollo – Fotolia.com

Published by JC Publications
ISBN: 9781547201358
Printed in the United States of America.

Table of Contents

Preface v

Chapter One 1
God's Friend

Chapter Two 13
Knowing God as Our Daddy

Chapter Three 47
Knowing God as Jesus Christ

Chapter Four 69
Knowing God as the Holy Spirit

Preface

For with the heart one believes unto righteousness, and with the mouth confession is made unto salvation (Romans 10:10).

The precious new birth that Jesus obtained for us is a two-step deal. We look at Romans 10:10 and say to ourselves, "If someone declares Jesus as their Lord, then they must mean it in their hearts." That is not necessarily so. For most people, that initial declaration is a statement of good intention. That covers the part about saying it with the mouth. We think in our minds that being born again is a good thing to do, and we'd like to do it, so we repeat a prayer out loud and consider ourselves to be born again.

However, there's a second step, which can operate at the same time as the good intention statement, but usually happens a bit later. That second step, the believing in the heart bit, actually means "total surrender." Is everyone willing to totally give themselves to the Lord? I think that's why there is usually a time distance between the two steps. Those with the good intentions need to prove God's love. Can they really trust Him?

The maxim "The road to hell is paved with good intentions," was given to a servant of God in an age gone by, and it has remained because it is a truism. A good intention is spoken out of the mouth. All of humanity is on the road to hell, and the only way to step off that road is through the precious new birth. That new birth is not complete until the person fully surrenders. Here's where people, though they have good intentions, continue on the road to hell. They don't believe in their hearts. Surrender is a heart move. Once they make that choice to fully surrender to the Lord, they step off the road to hell and step onto the highway to heaven.

There is still much work to be done in their souls: healing, deliverance, adding virtue, perseverance, love, etc. Happily, their new spirits are on the right road. The demons will try to hang on, but that road is also called the highway of holiness, and the demons, filthy as they are, can't stand that.

This book is to encourage those who have surrendered to the Lordship of Jesus, to instruct those who have good intentions but have not changed roads, and to entice those who are outside, who still wonder if it's all true. Only believe.

Chapter One

GOD'S FRIEND

So the LORD spoke to Moses face to face, as a man speaks to his friend . . . (Exodus 33:11).

Invariably when I speak about my relationship with God, people want to know if everybody is supposed to achieve that level of intimacy with Him. They think that somehow I have a closeness with the Lord that is not necessary for them, so they don't have it. Then I reflect on all the people I admire who have a much better friendship with Him than I have, and how I long to achieve their state. Yes. We should all be like Moses, speaking to Him face to face.

I have a hard time in social groups where everyone is speaking French. I must speak with a French person face to face to understand. Yet in the States where we do the same thing as the French, we all seem to speak at the same time, and even so, I understand all the various conversations going on around me. God understands everything everyone is saying all over the world at the same time, but He waits for the face to face. In normal conversation one person speaks, the other listens, and when the first one is finished the listener right away speaks. Not so with God. We speak to Him, and then He waits. He waits to see if we will really listen, or will we fill the empty gap with empty words.

"But you, Israel, are My servant, Jacob whom I have chosen, the descendants of Abraham My friend" (Isaiah 41:8).

We have to ask ourselves, are we God's friend? Do we know Him well enough to call Him friend? There is a big difference between knowing *about* somebody, and knowing that person directly, *face to face,* intimately. One can have story after story about someone, one can gather an armful of statistics, know all the facts of the person's life, but without the attachment that comes from one heart touching another heart, one does not know that person. And that is how it is with God. Unless we know Him on a familiar basis, quite informally, as a close friend, then we don't know Him. Friends share with one another and unless we share with Him what is on our heart, and receive what He has on His, then we don't know Him. We are not His friends.

The biggest barrier to intimacy with God is busyness. Our "To Do" lists dominate our lives. We think when we are in social situations, we must fill the air with words, little matter that they are meaningless. God does not fit Himself into our schedule, nor does He flail His way through all the words we use in order to speak to us. He waits. When we put our agenda aside, drop the list of things we want Him to do, are quiet before Him—quiet minds, quiet mouths, quiet bodies—and we focus on Him, then He is ready for relationship.

Recently, I watched a film entitled *Ali* (a movie about Muhammed Ali, formerly known as Cassius Clay, the world-champion boxer), and the star playing the role of Ali was one of my favorites, Will Smith. For an entire year, Will and the

GOD'S FRIEND

crew producing the movie, studied Muhammed Ali. Daily, Will ran for hours, took lessons in the Koran, studied the speech patterns of Ali, and reviewed films of the champion's body movements. He did exercises to train his body to be a champion, did mental exercises to realign his brain cells to think like a champion, and of course, he studied and practiced boxing. The result developed a fabulous film. But at no time did I think I was watching Muhammed Ali. I was well aware that Will Smith was playing a role. After that intensive study, all Will knew was *about* the man. He and Ali never shared the deepest secrets of their souls. Is that how we are with God? Well trained but no connection?

"No longer do I call you servants, for a servant does not know what his master is doing; but I have called you friends, for all things that I heard from My Father I have made known to you." (John 15:15).

Jesus tells us everything. Do we share our deepest secrets with Him? Do we think of God as our friend? Or do we follow a formula—a pattern of behavior, something that we memorize that makes us appear to be close to Him? Do we still think He is that angry being sitting on a heavenly throne throwing lightning bolts at us? Are we busy dodging His anger? Or do we engage ourselves in His life, His hopes and His dreams, as a friend would do? A true Christian is one who has surrendered his or her life for the sake of his or her friend, God.

"I have been crucified with Christ; it is no longer I who live, but Christ lives in me; and the life which I now live in the flesh I live by faith in the Son

of God, who loved me and gave Himself for me." (Galatians 2:20).

A real Christian is one who has submerged his or her life into Christ, who basically says, like Paul, "I'm dead. I no longer live. Christ is the one living in my body, and it is His life I now live, not mine." A true believer is someone who has died because he or she has passed through God's spiritual new birth. The life lived before is discarded in order to live new life after the new birth. Whatever we knew beforehand must pass away. We cannot tuck the new birth into our religious thinking and just keep operating like we did before. Life in Christ, after the new birth, is a life now being led by the Spirit of God.

And if Christ be in you, the body is dead because of sin; but the Spirit is life because of righteousness (Romans 8:10).

[13] *For if you live according to the flesh you will die; but if by the Spirit you put to death the deeds of the body, you will live.*

[14] *For as many as are led by the Spirit of God, these are sons of God* (Romans 8:13, 14).

The Spirit Himself bears witness with our spirit that we are children of God (Romans 8:16).

Nothing changes on this earth unless it is by the Spirit of God, and born-again Christians are the only ones who carry His Presence wherever we go. Without the Spirit of God, life goes on like it always has for generation after generation.

GOD'S FRIEND

Only the exterior changes to make the next generation think they are encountering something new.

The Israelites were terrified by the Presence of God; they didn't want Him to express Himself, so He complied with His beloved chosen and came to live in the synagogue in a box—an ark.

> [21] *"You shall put the mercy seat on top of the ark, and in the ark you shall put the Testimony that I will give you.*
>
> [22] *And there I will meet with you, and I will speak with you from above the mercy seat, from between the two cherubim which are on the ark of the Testimony, about everything which I will give you in commandment to the children of Israel."* (Exodus 25:21, 22).

But He didn't stay there. God stopped meeting with them at the Ark of the Covenant. Jeremiah spoke prophetically about that change.

> [15] *"And I will give you shepherds according to My heart, who will feed you with knowledge and understanding.*
>
> [16] *Then it shall come to pass, when you are multiplied and increased in the land in those days,"* says the LORD, *"that they will say no more, 'The ark of the covenant of the LORD.' It shall not come to mind, nor shall they remember it, nor shall they visit it, nor shall it be made anymore."* (Jeremiah 3:15, 16).

The Day came when the new birth provided new life, and that life was the Spirit of God coming to live inside each re-born person. No longer does God live in a box behind the altar. He lives in the living stones that make up His church: you and me. Some people live for popping pills, taking drugs to numb the pain, to avoid reality, or in hopes of heightening their senses or expand their understanding. They should try popping the living God into their lives, who has all power, which He gives to us who believe, who heals all the pain, no matter where it came from. They should try taking the Holy Spirit, who knows all and tells everything He knows to those of us who want to learn from Him. Some believe that as people gather around the communion table, they share the Presence of God, and when they walk away, they leave Him at the table to once again live in a box. They should expand their understanding and become the box He lives in!

When born-again Christians approach the communion table, they too, share the Presence of God in the holy meal, but when they walk away, they take Him with them. He never leaves them nor forsakes them. That is because we are the box God lives in. Now, perhaps, we can see the importance of knowing God! Everything depends on it! He works through us! It's not enough to know His voice; we must know His heart. We must be His friend.

Let's look at what the Bible says about knowing God:

And this is eternal life, that they may know You, the only true God, and Jesus Christ whom You have sent (John 17:3)***.***

If we receive Him, we will know God for eternity, and we will know Jesus Christ, because God sent Him.

GOD'S FRIEND

⁷ Beloved, let us love one another, for love is of God; and everyone who loves is born of God and knows God.

⁸ He who does not love does not know God, for God is love (1 John 4:7, 8).

To know God is to know love, because God is love.

And we know that the Son of God has come and has given us an understanding, that we may know Him who is true; and we are in Him who is true, in His Son Jesus Christ. This is the true God and eternal life (1 John 5:20).

Jesus came and gave us understanding about who God is. He is the true God. He is true, and Jesus is true, and we are in them.

In the beginning, God created Adam and Eve to be His best friends. He came to walk and talk with them in the cool of the evening. However, Adam did not value this friendship enough to honor it, and he gave away the authority and power over the earth that the Lord had given him. He gave it to Lucifer, the angel who rebelled against God, wanting to be god himself.

This dark angel came to Adam and Eve in the garden in the form of a snake, lying to them and promising what he could not provide. When these first two humans believed the lies, they died spiritually, and God no longer had direct access to their souls. Until Jesus came and gave us new spirits in the new birth, God spent His time proving to the Israelites that He was who He said He was. Throughout the Old Testament they had a hard time believing, perhaps because they were spiritually dead and could not talk to Him spirit to Spirit.

"I will take you as My people, and I will be your God. Then you shall know that I am the LORD your God who brings you out from under the burdens of the Egyptians" (Exodus 6:7).

> BORN-AGAIN CHRISTIANS, HOWEVER, HAVE NEW SPIRITS IN WHICH THE HOLY SPIRIT LIVES. WE WALK AND TALK WITH GOD WHENEVER WE WANT, BECAUSE HE IS ALWAYS INSIDE US!

Do you not know that you are the temple of God and that the Spirit of God dwells in you (1 Corinthians 3:16)?

There are a few things we need to know about God, in general, before we begin our specific study.

GOD HEARS US.

"Now we know that God does not hear sinners; but if anyone is a worshiper of God and does His will, He hears him." (John 9:31).

Notice the two qualifications that we must meet for God to hear us: we must be a worshiper of God, and we must do His will—not our own. God is enormous! He fills the Universe! If all seven billion people on the earth prayed at the same time, He would hear every prayer in whatever language the pray-er would use! Not only that, He knows every

GOD'S FRIEND

thought each of the seven billion people think! He's HUGE! So please note: He can choose who He listens to!

GOD DEMANDS PROOF OF OUR FRIENDSHIP.

We know how God tested Abraham by requiring him to sacrifice his son, Isaac, on an altar on the Mount of Moriah, or as we know it—Mount Zion. Abraham was stopped before the knife could cut Isaac's throat, but the quality of Abraham's friendship with God was tested in that way. We also know that God tested the Israelites under the guidance of Moses.

And you shall remember that the LORD your God led you all the way these forty years in the wilderness, to humble you and test you, to know what was in your heart, whether you would keep His commandments or not (Deuteronomy 8:2).

⁸ *"And it shall come to pass in all the land," Says the LORD, "That two-thirds in it shall be cut off and die, but one-third shall be left in it:*

⁹ *I will bring the one-third through the fire, will refine them as silver is refined, and test them as gold is tested. They will call on My name, And I will answer them. I will say, 'This is My people'; And each one will say, 'The LORD is my God'"* (Zechariah 13:8, 9).

We can expect to be tested, not just for Him, but for our own sakes so we can see how much further we have to go to be one He listens to attentively, and to whom we listen attentively. We *choose* to obey! We *choose* to worship! The one whose life will change will be ours!

GOD LEADS US INTO CHANGE.

He accepts us as we are, loving us in whatever condition we are in, but He loves us too much to leave us in that condition. He immediately starts changing things. It's almost like the Holy Spirit does house cleaning, rearranging the furniture to make it comfortable for Him to live in us.

Or do you despise the riches of His goodness, forbearance, and longsuffering, not knowing that the goodness of God leads you to repentance (Romans 2:4)?

Whatever change the Holy Spirit requires, do it! He knows us better than we know ourselves, so follow Him, trust Him, and obey Him.

GOD CONFIDES IN US, AND HE LISTENS TO US AND COMPLIES WITH OUR REQUESTS.

We have a God who works in our behalf, and who wants us to have the desires of our hearts, after all, He is the one who put those desires in our hearts. Other religions require the adherents to work for their god and that artificial god does not have the power to give desires to the people.

And He said to them, "To you it has been given to know the mystery of the kingdom of God; but to

GOD'S FRIEND

those who are outside, all things come in parables" (Mark 4:11).

"But even now I know that whatever You ask of God, God will give You" (John 11:22).

John, in one of his little books, said that God answered every prayer he prayed. I'd like to have that happen for me, too.

And whatever we ask we receive from Him, because we keep His commandments and do those things that are pleasing in His sight (1 John 3:22).

Keeping His commandments is doing His will, and things that are pleasing in His sight include worshipping Him.

GOD IS FAITHFUL.

There are too many Scriptures about God being faithful to even enumerate them, so I've only listed three which indicate the power of His faithfulness. Thank God He is faithful!

God is faithful, by whom you were called into the fellowship of His Son, Jesus Christ our Lord (1 Corinthians 1:9).

If we are faithless, He remains faithful; He cannot deny Himself (2 Timothy 2:13).

Let us hold fast the confession of our hope without wavering, for He who promised is faithful (Hebrews 10:23).

Chapter Two
KNOWING GOD AS OUR DADDY

Knowing these five basic elements helps us to know God better.

1. God hears us.
2. God demands proof of our friendship.
3. God leads us into change.
4. God confides in us, and He listens to us and complies.
5. God is faithful.

The place to start is to know Him as Father. He is a loving Father. We cannot separate God from Love because that is His substance. He cannot do anything but love. After Adam turned away, God still came to the earth to walk and talk with His Creation, but fewer and fewer people wanted to walk and talk with Him. Looking at how the Israelites rebelled in just about everything, one can see they wanted to be their own gods. They wanted to be in charge.

In the Old Testament, the word *father* is used 630 times. Only nine of those verses call God "Father." Of these nine verses, five are prophetic words of who God would be to

Jesus; three verses are rebukes to the Israelites for not honoring their Creator; one is a declaration by God that He will be a father to Solomon.

And he said unto me, Solomon thy son, he shall build my house and my courts: for I have chosen him to be my son, and I will be his father (1 Chronicles 28:6).

I find this verse to be intriguing. This is our heavenly Father speaking, and Solomon is the only one in the Old Testament of whom God says He will be his father. The Lord promised David his seed would be kings forever. Jesus was born in David's bloodline; Matthew and Luke prove the lineage of Jesus, one through Joseph and one through Mary. We know Jesus to be King of kings. But who are we? We are kings and priests because we are in Jesus' line. We are sons and daughters just like Solomon, and we are, today, building houses and courts for God Almighty by inviting others to become living stones in His temple, more "boxes" God will live in.

Jesus did not have physical seed in natural children; He has spiritual seed in spiritual children. He has provided the new birth. That positions us to be just like Solomon, with God as our Father, as we ask for wisdom to rule and reign in our lifetimes.

For if by the one man's offense death reigned through the one, much more those who receive abundance of grace and of the gift of righteousness will reign in life through the One, Jesus Christ.

[17] ***For if by the one man's offense death reigned through the one, much more those who receive***

KNOWING GOD AS OUR DADDY

abundance of grace and of the gift of righteousness will reign in life through the One, Jesus Christ.)

[18] *Therefore, as through one man's offense judgment came to all men, resulting in condemnation, even so through one Man's righteous act the free gift came to all men, resulting in justification of life.*

[19] *For as by one man's disobedience many were made sinners, so also by one Man's obedience many will be made righteous.*

[20] *Moreover the law entered that the offense might abound. But where sin abounded, grace abounded much more,*

[21] *so that as sin reigned in death, even so grace might reign through righteousness to eternal life through Jesus Christ our Lord* (Romans 5:17–21).

In the New Testament, there are 325 verses that use the word *father*. Of those 325 verses, 236 call God "Father." None of them are prophetic verses telling us who He will be, rather they are here and now verses of who He is today—our Heavenly Father.

Of the 236 verses, 33 specifically call God "Our Father," meaning yours and mine. We can clearly see from all these references that Jesus brought a very personal, intimate understanding of God—that He is now our Daddy.

I used to say that if someone wanted to know God, they should study all the names used for Him in the Old Testament: *Jehovah Jireh, Jehovah Rapha, Jehovah Shammah, Jehovah Tsidkenu, Jehovah Rohi,* and so on. The Jews were certainly well instructed in what God does by all the names that were

15

used to describe Him. Today I say, if someone wants to know God, they should read John's writings in the New Testament. In his Gospel, John uses the word *father* in 110 verses. Of those 110, 103 refer to God as "Father." In one of his little books, John explains our spiritual growth pattern:

> [12] ***I write to you, little children, because your sins are forgiven you for His name's sake.***
>
> [13] ***I write to you, fathers, because you have known Him who is from the beginning. I write to you, young men, because you have overcome the wicked one. I write to you, little children, because you have known the Father.***
>
> [14] ***I have written to you, fathers, because you have known Him who is from the beginning. I have written to you, young men, because you are strong, and the word of God abides in you, and you have overcome the wicked one*** (1 John 2:12–14).

We are first "little children." Someone who knows the Father like a little child knows their sins are forgiven, and they know God as their Daddy. I never had a Daddy, so I was thrilled to know God as my Daddy. Let's allow the Bible to further explain this spiritual level of "little children."

> ***For you did not receive the spirit of bondage again to fear, but you received the Spirit of adoption by whom we cry out, "Abba, Father."*** (Romans 8:15).

On one of my visits to Israel, I took a bus from the home I stayed in to the Holocaust museum, and I observed an Israeli family getting off at a bus stop. The father and the mother,

KNOWING GOD AS OUR DADDY

plus four little children stepped down and turned off to the right, but the last little boy was looking to the left, and when he stepped off the bus he couldn't see his family.

In a great panic he shouted "*Abba*! *Abba*! *Abba*!" The father turned toward him, knelt down, and spread his arms wide open, into which the little boy ran with great relief. That was, for me, a most poignant demonstration of my Father God's "Daddyhood." It also confirmed to me that the word *Abba* actually means "Daddy."

After we grow up a little more, we become young people; we have learned to overcome the devil. We know how to take authority over him, such as I did when I cut my finger. As a young housewife, I wanted to be thrifty and please my husband, yet provide my growing children with protein for their developing muscles, so I bought a hunk of cheap meat. As I started to cut it into cubes to make a stew, I was surprised to find how tough it was. It was so sinewy that I had to take out a serrated knife and saw at it as if it were a piece of wood!

As I worked, I heard it cutting on a bone. I frowned; I didn't buy a piece of meat with bones in it. I kept sawing away. But when I saw the bright red blood flowing out from underneath the piece of meat, I realized I was cutting on my own bone. My grip had been so tight I could not feel what was happening to my finger. I dropped the meat, the knife went skittering across the floor, and I drew my hand up to my face where I watched my blood spurting across the kitchen. Panicking, I grabbed my finger to put pressure on the cut, which was the only thing I knew to do.

But then I heard a little voice inside me. "You don't have to put up with this."

My mind responded, "Yes, I do. I did it to myself." Fortunately, I did not speak these words, but I didn't know what else to do, so I stood in my kitchen squeezing my finger in front of my face.

The voice spoke again, "Tell it to close up."

I screamed at that finger, "In the name of Jesus Christ you close up!"

Then the voice said, "Now let go of your finger."

My mind was doing multiple somersaults. "What? What was that? Let go?"

I obeyed. Slowly, the fingers on my uncut hand released their grip. The blood had stopped squirting, and as I watched, the cut closed up before my eyes. I wasn't even left with a scar. The only evidence I had was my blood still dripping down my cabinet doors.

When I shouted at that finger, I was taking authority over a piece of work the devil did—a piece of work the devil tried to blame on me. As we grow up, we learn that anytime anything goes wrong, the devil is to blame. He is behind everything that prevents us from having God's best. As we grow up, we also become strong, and the devil gets by with less and less. The Word of God is in us because we have read it, studied it, spoken it, and believed it, and we use it against the devil, just like Jesus did when He was tempted in the desert.

Then as adults, as *fathers*, which means "mature people," we know God. We know Him on a very personal level. As a grown-up, we don't send other people to speak to God for us. If my best friend sent someone to speak to me on their behalf, I would be insulted. My friend should know they can come to me directly. I don't need an intermediary to express

KNOWING GOD AS OUR DADDY

my friend's desires. Only children, or immature Christians, need an intermediary.

As Christians, we cannot be satisfied with people coming between us and God, our Daddy. Nor does God want someone to intervene for us. He wants to see us face to face. The only way to get to that place is to wait on Him. In the beginning, this kind of praying takes exercise. Our senses do not want to cooperate. To wait on the Lord means we get ourselves into a quiet state where our minds are not running at 90 kilometers an hour, talking, talking, talking. Our emotions are calm, unruffled, whereas normally our emotions like a little action, lifting us up and down, spinning us around, making mountains out of molehills, as we say in the States.

Someone once asked Smith Wigglesworth how he felt, and he answered sharply, "I don't ask myself how I feel. I tell myself how to feel." That's basically what we do when we wait on the Lord, we tell our minds and emotions how to behave, to be quiet and to wait. Then when we reach that state of waiting, we begin to feel the Holy Spirit rising up big on the inside of us. Sometimes a rush of tears comes to my eyes, sometimes a warmth cocoons me, or a flood of tongues erupts from inside, and I find myself singing love songs to the Lord. From that point on, He is in charge of the prayer, and I flow wherever He goes.

When that kind of prayer is over, a big sigh comes out of me, and I open my eyes. I know that whatever I was praying for is now an accomplished fact, and I write in my journal everything I saw and heard so that later, when I see things happening in the natural realm, I can understand what happened in the prayer.

When I lived just outside of Montpellier, I decided I wanted to hear from the Lord—not for something I was asking for—I just wanted to hear whatever He wanted to say to me, so I set myself to wait on Him. I sat in my living room on a little sofa for two, my laptop tucked underneath the sofa. Through a double sliding glass window, I looked onto a lovely stretch of grass, a swimming pool, tall bushes to hide the street and the tiled roofs of the houses beyond. My mind fought me with all its strength.

"Are you going to sit there all day and get nothing done?"

I told it to be quiet, and that I was waiting on the Lord.

"Well, if by the end of the day, nothing has been accomplished, don't blame me! Don't you realize all the work you have to do?"

Sometimes, I have to be really tough with my mind, and this was one of those times. "SHUT UP!"

"Don't you tell me to shut up! I know what I'm talking about!"

"You will obey me! We are waiting on the Lord!"

"You need to stay on target, and sitting around like this is not getting your job done."

But while this dialogue continued, I noticed that the grass, the swimming pool, the tall hedge, the houses across the street had all disappeared, and only a dirt path extended from my sliding glass door. Way in the distance I could see a tiny figure walking toward me. So of course, my attention was drawn to this, yet I kept up the dispute with my mind. As the figure came closer, the discourse with my mind took less and less importance as I wondered who the figure was and what were the funny clothes he was wearing.

KNOWING GOD AS OUR DADDY

When I realized it was Jesus, my mind shut up completely. My Lord wore a bridegroom's outfit from ancient times, breeches buckled at the knee, an ornate vest with a white shirt underneath whose sleeves bloomed out, stockings, and buckled shoes with pointed toes. He came and offered me His right hand. I took it with my left, realizing He wanted me to stand, and when I looked down, I saw I was wearing a white bridal gown. He said not a word but led me down the path He had just come from, and we walked in a stately manner. Then I saw we were headed for the throne room.

Upon arrival God, my Father, extended His left hand to me, which I took with my right hand. He drew me onto His left knee. This was surprising; every other time I had visited the throne room I was given His right hand, and I sat on His right knee. I knew, by now, that God does nothing that is out of order, so I waited to know the meaning of this left knee experience. I noticed that the crown I wore had five spokes extending from it, and they had entered God's cheek, but He didn't seem to be concerned.

He whispered some things in my ear. Then He indicated Jesus, who still stood at the bottom of the four steps to the throne. He extended His right hand to me, and I took it with my left. I rose, and we walked around to the right side of the throne. There I saw a throne I had never seen before, and I knew it was the throne of Jesus. We walked up the four steps, and we both sat on Jesus' throne. God was now in the center, Jesus on His right, and I was to the right of Jesus. We were all in our proper places.

Which He worked in Christ when He raised Him from the dead and seated Him at His right hand in the heavenly places, (Ephesians 1:20).

⁴ But God, who is rich in mercy, because of His great love with which He loved us,

⁵ even when we were dead in trespasses, made us alive together with Christ (by grace you have been saved),

⁶ and raised us up together, and made us sit together in the heavenly places in Christ Jesus, (Ephesians 2:4–6).

I sat there for a minute, and then God leaned around His Son and nodded for me to do what I was supposed to do. I decreed and declared before the heavenly angels what God had whispered in my ear, and they rushed off to accomplish it. Jesus stood, took my hand, and I stood with Him. We went down the steps and took the path back to my two-seat sofa. About halfway there I could hear God my Father calling and I looked back. He had come to the edge of the dais to call after me. "Go ahead and write for the internet." As it had been on my heart to do just that, I could now hardly wait to get back to that sofa.

When I arrived, I quickly pulled my laptop from underneath and began writing. But then I had the weird feeling someone was in the room, and I looked around to find Jesus still there, standing behind me, only this time He was in working clothes, just His ordinary white robe, white belt around His waist and His sandals. Surprised I asked, "Do You want to go someplace else?"

KNOWING GOD AS OUR DADDY

He nodded. He still had not said one word to me throughout this whole vision. I put the laptop aside, stood up and was startled to see that I had on my working clothes—jeans and a tee-shirt. I took His hand, and instead of walking straight ahead, we turned right and walked through the wall of my apartment. There at our feet was a large abyss that stretched either side as far as the eye could see. Angry fire raged in the bottom of the abyss. People were in there, and they tried desperately to climb out, but the sides were straight up and down. One man made it to the edge and just as he reached for the foot of Jesus, he fell back in.

Jesus looked at me and said, "Your writing keeps people from coming here." Then I found myself alone, in my apartment, my laptop on my lap.

This prayer experience was, of course, very dramatic for me, so I wanted to write it up as evidence of what can happen in a prayer time called "Waiting On The Lord." If we are going to become spiritual adults, then we must be willing to have adult spiritual experiences. We must know Him and be His friend.

Years ago, before going to Rhema, I was heavily involved in a Christian work called "Camps Farthest Out," a charismatic group who would meet in the summer and go to remote places in order to pray as "far out" as they could get. Some of the speakers became very good friends of mine, and they shared their trials with their son, a grown man, who was getting deeper and deeper into drugs. Finally, their son arrived at a point where if someone had not intervened medically, he would have overdosed and killed himself.

Totally distraught, they sought the help of a pastor for whom they were speaking. He advised them in this manner:

he pledged his church to be the prayer support they needed; his congregation would do all the praying and they could go on about their business of being traveling teachers. They needn't bother to pray.

When they told me this, I had a sharp feeling in my spirit that this wouldn't work at all. I didn't know much at the time, but what I did know did not agree with this pastor. I told my friends of my angst about them turning their son's difficulties over to this church, but they considered me to be a baby Christian and paid no attention. The last I heard about this man was ten years ago, and he was still a druggie, in and out of jail, in and out of rehabilitation centers.

I've since discovered spiritual protocol which explained what I was feeling back then. Parents have spiritual authority over their children only until they come of age, which happens sometime after puberty. Let's just say fifteen is the average age. At that point of growth, the child should have learned enough about God to make his or her own prayers. However, these parents should have prayed, as well as the church members, as they were the closest to their son and felt the most intensity about his condition. We can all pray for anybody we want to, but the passion of our prayer is the key to it's being answered. Passion for God, passion for His works, passion for His righteousness, passion for the request. It's important that the person being prayed for gives his or her permission for the pray-er to pray as God will not countermand our free-will. In this case, the son was not consulted. The church should have asked the Lord what to do, and probably He would have told them to intervene with the young man directly. God does not seem to appreciate prayers that we initiate on our own, asking Him to do what we think

KNOWING GOD AS OUR DADDY

ought to be done. We are to seek the Kingdom of God first, and find out what God thinks ought to be done, and then pray for that. He has an answer for everything.

People can help, but they cannot take the place of our faith. Christianity is an internal relationship with God, a very intimate, personal relationship that no one else can build for us. All relationships are built, and our relationship with God is built step by step, love by love.

When I received my new birth, I fell madly in love with God. He is madly in love with us, by the way. Some friends from the States came to France for a visit, and I arranged for us to housesit for some other friends who needed to go back to the States for a while. The visiting friends were ones with whom I pray a lot, and so we passed most of our time in the lovely home, praying. During one session, I found myself on the floor.

I muttered over and over, "You are everything to me. You are everything to me. You are everything to me." Then I reduced it to, "You are everything. You are everything. You are everything." It went further, "You are. You are. You are." And finally, "You. You. You." Then I was quiet. There was nothing else to say. In the stillness I heard Him say, "You are everything to Me." His love for us is profound, all-encompassing, forever, magnificent, majestic, thorough, complete, and overwhelmingly wonderful. If we know Him as a spiritual adult, we will know Him in His love for us.

Let me go back to the beginning. Immediately upon receiving Jesus as Lord, I was happy to be born again! I wanted to know everything. I went to every church meeting I could find, and I listened in on people's conversations so I could learn what they knew. I heard people saying, "The other day when I was talking to the Lord, ..." Or "The Lord spoke to me and said, ..." I wanted to know how to do that, so I began asking questions.

"How can you hear the voice of God?"

People would look at me kind of funny and say, "I don't know. I just hear Him."

"How do you know it's God's voice you are hearing?"

They'd shrug and say, "I don't know. I just know it's Him."

Finally, a little old lady pulled me aside and said, "Listen, honey, we all hear hundreds of voices in our heads, but only one voice is full of love. Even when He is angry with you, His voice is still full of love. You can hear love in a voice, and you can hear when that person doesn't love you, even if they are doing their best to sound like they do. Now you go home and listen to the voices in your head. When you can figure out which one is full of love for you, that's the Lord. Then you'll be home free, and you'll know which voice to follow."

I went home and sat in the quiet of my living room. No one else was home, kids were at school, husband at work, and our walls were thick as the house had been built in 1906 when they were still making sturdy houses. At first I heard nothing. Then I realized I was so accustomed to hearing those voices that they no longer made an impression on my conscious mind. Slowly, the individual sounds came through clearly. There was the doctor who brought my two children to birth. He was still ordering me to walk 30 minutes a day. There was my third-grade teacher, still telling me to sit up straight. My mother. My father. My sisters. And what was that? Aha! The one voice that loved me. He wasn't any

KNOWING GOD AS OUR DADDY

louder than the others. He wasn't any more authoritative. His voice was just the same as the streaming of the others, but it was full of love. Overflowing with love.

Now I knew who to follow, and if I chose to follow His voice, I could never be blindsided again. Human beings that we are, we can still make some pretty bad choices even when we know His voice, and I am no exception. There are times when I do follow my reasoning instead of my instruction from the Lord, but when that decision brings me to a crushing failure, I turn around to see that the Lord is still standing there with the wise advice He had to give in the first place. He is always faithful.

> [1] *"Most assuredly, I say to you, he who does not enter the sheepfold by the door, but climbs up some other way, the same is a thief and a robber*
>
> [2] *But he who enters by the door is the shepherd of the sheep.*
>
> [3] *To him the doorkeeper opens, and the sheep hear his voice; and he calls his own sheep by name and leads them out.*
>
> [4] *And when he brings out his own sheep, he goes before them; and the sheep follow him, for they know his voice.*
>
> [5] *Yet they will by no means follow a stranger, but will flee from him, for they do not know the voice of strangers"* (John 10:1–5).
>
> [27] *"My sheep hear My voice, and I know them, and they follow Me.*

> [28] *And I give them eternal life, and they shall never perish; neither shall anyone snatch them out of My hand.*
>
> [29] *My Father, who has given them to Me, is greater than all; and no one is able to snatch them out of My Father's hand.*
>
> [30] *I and My Father are one."* (John 10:27–30).

It is imperative that we know His voice. We recognize every other voice that is important to us: our spouses, our children, our parents, our close friends, etc. Shouldn't His voice be the most important: that of our Creator, our Provider, our Savior, our Lord? He says we will know His voice, and we will follow Him.

My son took a trip to Israel with his class from Bible School, and the tour guide stopped the bus at the bottom of a hill. He told the students to wait just a few minutes and they would see something extraordinary. Soon five flocks of sheep came over the crest of the hill lead by five shepherds. The men were singing and clearly the sheep that belonged to each flock were gathered around the voice they knew. The tour guide said the shepherds led the sheep everyday across the hill and their appearance deftly expressed what Jesus meant when He said His sheep would know His voice and follow Him. The Bible says He sings over us.

In exactly the same fashion of wanting to know His voice, I heard people talking about being in the Spirit, and I wanted that, whatever it was. This time I knew better than to ask anybody, because I knew they wouldn't know what to say. So, I asked the Lord, "How do I get into the Spirit?"

KNOWING GOD AS OUR DADDY

He said to start by using my imagination. Imagine I was swimming in heavy air. So, I saw myself swimming down my street, about ten feet high, and I admired all the Victorian houses I passed. Then He told me to look up and see the underside of a manhole cover. I looked up, and I saw what He meant. He said to swim up to it; so, I did. He told me to slide the manhole cover to the side and climb out. I did.

When I was about halfway out, my imagination stopped, and my spiritual vision took over. How do I know this was not my imagination? Because I could not have imagined what happened next. In pure, white light, with nothing of any shape or contour around me, I pulled myself out and stood by the open manhole while drops of heavy air fell from my clothing. Out of nowhere two angels swooped up from behind, each one took an arm, and they flew me at the speed of light across the expanse of heaven, and suddenly set me down on my feet.

I have no idea what I stood on because I intently looked forward and saw what I assumed to be the Throne Room of God Almighty. He languidly sat at a 90-degree angle to me on His throne on a platform, reached by four steps. The throne, dais, and steps were solid gold. He, however, although distinct, seemed to be made of fire.

He turned and said, "Come to me." That appeal made me want to run and jump in His arms, fire or no fire. I looked down to see if there was something I could walk on to get to Him and was astonished to see that I was dressed like a three-year-old, which was accurate for my spiritual age at the time. I had on little black patent leather shoes we used to call "Mary Janes," and a dress with a puffy skirt. It was kind of a teal color. The angels pushed me forward, and they stayed behind. I climbed the four steps like a three-year-old would do, since the steps were of a size a three-year-old would have a hard time managing.

God picked me up, sat me on His right knee and said, "Tell me about yourself." I thought He knew all about me, but it seemed important to Him to hear it from me, so I told Him. When I cried over my troubles on the earth, He cried with me. When I laughed over my joys on the earth, He laughed with me. Then He told me how to handle my troubles.

When we finished talking, He said, "Now you have been to my Throne Room, and you can come here anytime you want. I'm always here. I always have time for you." Then I was back in my bedroom on Green Street in San Francisco. Since then I have made many trips to the Throne Room, but I've also made many trips to the Spirit realm without dropping into the Throne Room. I'm welcome to investigate and learn, the angels help and protect me, and I no longer have to use my imagination. I don't have to travel through the manhole. All I do is desire to go there, and I'm there.

[7] Because the carnal mind is enmity against God; for it is not subject to the law of God, nor indeed can be.

[8] So then, those who are in the flesh cannot please God.

[9] But you are not in the flesh but in the Spirit, if indeed the Spirit of God dwells in you. Now if anyone does not have the Spirit of Christ, he is not His.

KNOWING GOD AS OUR DADDY

‍¹⁰ And if Christ is in you, the body is dead because of sin, but the Spirit is life because of righteousness.

¹¹ But if the Spirit of Him who raised Jesus from the dead dwells in you, He who raised Christ from the dead will also give life to your mortal bodies through His Spirit who dwells in you (Romans 8:7–11).

Finding out who our Father is, means finding out who we are. He created us for His pleasure. What is His pleasure? In seeking His face, we will find our destiny, that for which we were predestined to do. That which makes His face to shine upon us!

In Him also we have obtained an inheritance, being predestined according to the purpose of Him who works all things according to the counsel of His will (Ephesians 1:11).

From the first day I learned to hear His voice, my Father repeatedly said to me, "Write for Me." "I love your writing." "You were created to write." I had wanted to be a writer all my life. The little diary I wrote in as a twelve-year-old had this entry: "Today I sent two manuscripts to Reader's Digest." Of course, they didn't publish them; that entry simply shows how early my desire started.

When I left for the university, my parents told me I must major in Home Economics, and since they were paying the bill, I signed up for that, but I only took writing classes. The school placed me in accelerated English classes, invited me to join the exclusive Honorary Poetry Society, made me literary editor of the yearbook and hired me to write their handbooks. They recognized the gift in me.

After two years, my mother and stepfather sat me down for counsel. They wanted to know why I didn't take any Home Economic classes. My mother asked what I wanted to do when I finished school, and I told them I wanted to be a journalist.

My mother was awe-struck. She asked, "Whoever told you that you could write? You're not intelligent enough to be a writer." They had a few more discouraging words to say, and then I asked them what they thought I could do (with my limited intelligence). My mother reminded me that I had swum across Lake Calhoun at midnight the other night; maybe I could teach sports. Fortunately, I liked athletics. The degree I obtained from the university allowed me to teach school at the level of the twelve to fourteen-year-olds. Following my parent's advice, I put away all my writings and took no more English, or Drama, or Creative Writing classes. I quit the Honorary Poetry Society and stopped writing for the school.

I was forty years old before I started writing again, right after I heard the Lord say He created me to write. Hey! If it was His idea, who could stand against Him? If He wanted me to write, then I must be capable of doing so. However, I stalled, because all those negative words about my ability kept ringing in my head. Eleven years after my new birth, I attended a meeting with 10,000 other Christians, and the preacher had an altar call for those in the ministry who felt like square pegs in round holes. That was me. I was pastoring at the time and really enjoying myself, but I knew it was not where I belonged. I decided that even if I were the only one to answer that call, I had to go down front.

KNOWING GOD AS OUR DADDY

There were so many of us that we were squashed together in front of that altar. I heard only one word, and it was shouted at me by God. He said, "Write!" Now God is our Daddy, and fathers get tired of telling their children what to do; when they don't do it, fathers have been known to shout! That's what my Father did. And suddenly, I knew what to do!

I knew to write short stories and put them on the radio. Strange as that seemed to me, because I never listened to the radio, and still don't today, I went home and got started. I collected people's testimonies of what Jesus had done in their lives, made short stories out of them, and then recorded them on cassette tapes (yes, it was a long time ago!) Those cassette tapes were sent to seven Christian radio stations, and one responded with very glad news.

They invited me to put my stories on their station; they taught me how to do all the mechanics of the task, and they gave me unlimited use of their studios! I was thrilled. Not only was I at the task the Lord had given to me, I discovered I had a natural "radio voice." Everything went exceedingly well for many months, but the day came when I didn't have the money to pay for putting my programs on their station.

When I called and told the director I must cancel my contract, he said, "Oh, that's too bad." We hung up after agreeing that I would record for two more weeks, and that would be the end. The next day he called me. "We had an emergency board meeting last night, and we decided you can be on our station for as long as you want for free. You are reaching the lost, and they don't know they must send in offerings to pay for the radio programs." What joy!

Then the Lord told me to merge my church with a friend of mine who had a lovely church in the same city not far away. He told me to take my stories to the churches. In fact, He gave me the names of three churches in my town to contact. I was certain that no pastor would want to give up his Sunday morning pulpit in order for his congregation to listen to stories. To my astonishment, all three pastors said yes. It went very well. I discovered I was a natural story-teller.

One of the pastors and I had a mutual friend on the other side of the United States who also pastored a fine church. He called our friend and told him about my stories. That pastor invited me to fly out and tell stories to his congregation, which I did. Since we were good friends, I stayed a week with them, and his wife asked me to accompany her to an appointment—she hosted a live radio program. She contended that my stories were pre-recorded, and I had never experienced live radio, which I should at least see.

As my friend prepared herself behind the microphone, I sat against the wall admiring all the very modern and expensive equipment. Suddenly, the station manager pulled a microphone down from the ceiling and positioned it directly in front of my mouth. I asked, "What's this for?"

She said, "Why, you're our featured guest today."

I gasped, "I am?"

She asked, "Have you ever done live radio?"

I whimpered, "No!"

She said, "Oh, you'll love it! We're on in 30 seconds."

I looked desperately at my friend, "What do I do?"

She laughed, "Tell your stories, of course!" So for one hour, I told my stories, and it was great fun knowing I was speaking directly to the audience.

KNOWING GOD AS OUR DADDY

Afterwards the manager came back into the studio and said, "We loved those! Can we put them on our station every week for free?"

Free! The word resonated in my soul. "Absolutely!"

She gave me a big smile, "You don't know who we are, do you?"

"You're a little local station with some beautiful equipment. That's all I know."

She laughed. "Our mother station is in Australia. We beam our programs to them, and they beam them to the entire world."

The entire world! Only God could have orchestrated that. This continued for many years, until the rich gentleman who financed this world-wide radio, died. His death changed everything as his family decided to close down his philanthropic endeavors. This was a big blow to Christian radio. At the same time, the little radio station that jump-started me had been sold to a nation-wide rock and roll station. They didn't want my stories.

During this same period, I returned to France, alone, again as a missionary but somewhat misguided. I wanted to work with a certain British couple who gladly received my request to share in their ministry. However, they left two weeks before my return. They took the car they planned for me to drive; they left me with the rent to pay for three more months on a large house, and a list of their friends to call in order to minister to them. I called all these people the minute I read the note. My suitcases still sat by the front door. Their friends were British and had no desire to include an American in their lives, spiritually or non-spiritually, and on the first day of my arrival, I found myself without friends and no place to minister.

Just as a little self-pity started climbing up inside of me, I heard a knock at the door. I answered to find two French women on my doorstep. The real estate agent in town (who I didn't know, nor had ever met) told them I was a Bible teacher; they wanted to know if I would teach them the Bible. The following day we had our first Bible study, and by the end of the week I had five Bible studies in five villages nearby. As time passed, the numbers grew; when there were thirty-five of us, I also started a church on Sunday nights in an empty restaurant.

I made friends with the local Catholic Deacon and together we invited Protestants and Catholics to join us for a dinner of Unity at a local restaurant. The evening turned out to be a roaring success, and after that, I moved the church to this restaurant, which was normally closed on Sunday evening. I also made friends with other pastors in the area, and one was in the process of gathering all the little churches, like mine, under his umbrella of organization. I joined. And then he took the church away from me. Overnight I went from being an up-and-coming pastor to being bereft of all contacts in the area.

I lay on the floor of my living room and shook. I didn't know what to do! Alone. Completely alone. What could I tell the people back home? When others are supporting you, every move you make is important; you are on display. What could I say to them? Where was God?

He let me shake for three days, and then He quietly spoke. "You did everything that pastor asked you to do, didn't you?"

KNOWING GOD AS OUR DADDY

I said, "Yes."
"And nothing worked out, did it?"
I said, "No."
"You did everything your husband wanted you to do, didn't you?"
I said, "Yes."
"And nothing worked out, did it?"
I said, "No."
Then He very quietly asked, "Why don't you do what I want you to do and see if that doesn't work out for you?"

By this time my despondency had me so disoriented, I didn't know what He wanted from me. I started crying again, "What do You want me to do?"

"Write, of course! Pull out all those stories you put on the radio in English, have them translated and put them on the air over here."

I pulled them out, had them translated, but my French was laughable from the standpoint of recording it. My friend, who led praise and worship in my church, called to re-establish our friendship, and I asked him to record my stories for the radio. His wife became my narrator, and he became the technician, as well as the musician and sound effects guy. One night there was a knock on the door, I opened it, and he shoved a cassette in my hands, turned, and left without saying a word.

I put the cassette in the player and sat down to listen. It took my breath away. My friends had taken my black and white words on plain paper and made of them a symphony in full color. Her voice was perfect; his music was powerful; the sound effects were dramatic. I slipped from the sofa to the floor, tears dropping onto the carpet in awe and thanksgiving.

On the internet I found sixteen Christian radio stations. I sent copies of that cassette to the sixteen and fervently prayed, "Oh, Father, please let me have just one station." Fifteen said yes. For the next ten years, I built up the output of my stories to 107 stations in various French speaking countries around the world. Not one of them asked me to pay for airtime. In fact, several sent checks to encourage me. At the end, over twelve million people were actively listening to my stories.

I offered to put my address and phone number on the air after one of my stories was heard, but management was always against it. "That's too American. We do it differently. We ask the listeners to call us so that we can recommend local churches." That was fine by me, seeing as my spoken French was so inadequate. All I was interested in was to have the listeners taken care of.. It meant I had very little contact with the stations except to send in my story for the week. However, a station manager called me. He said he thought I would like to know what was happening at his station. (The range of his signal reached over a million people.) One night, a beleaguered volunteer, the only one on duty, didn't listen to the programs playing as she had been left with too much work to do. The listeners heard one of my stories entitled The Good Samaritan.

A listener called and asked the volunteer what that man had done who was a patient in The Good Samaritan hospital. She confessed she didn't know because she hadn't the time to listen. The caller said he was desperate to know because

KNOWING GOD AS OUR DADDY

he, too, like the character, had terminal cancer and he wanted to overcome his cancer like the character did in the story.

She apologized for not having an answer for him. As she reflected how to help this caller, an idea came to her to take the station off the automatic programming. Then she would announce to the listening audience that a caller needed to know what the character in the story did, as he had terminal cancer and wanted to do the same thing. She told them she would now replay the story called The Good Samaritan. That way the caller could take notes on what to do to overcome his cancer.

The station manager said the volunteer did just that, and for the last two months the station had received over 200 calls of people thanking them for re-playing the story, because now they were healed. The healings were of all varieties of ills, not just of cancer. And yes, six weeks after the re-play, the man who made the initial call called again to report he had been totally healed of the terminal cancer.

Things change over a period of ten years. My friends' lives became more involved, and they no longer had time to produce my stories for radio. At the same time, I was introduced to a studio in Paris who took up the work. I moved to Paris to be near the studio, and in time to attend a national congress of owners and directors of Christian radio stations. At this convention, a sympathetic owner took me aside and confided that all stations were now consolidating with him and his new format. He had just won some honors for his station, and everyone was clamoring to join him. After today, that congress, which I had been attending for eight years, would no longer exist. He was forming something new.

He asked with perfect sincerity, "Will you please write stories in a two-minute format? Other than songs, nothing we do will last over 2 minutes." I tried the two-minute format and failed. I'm a dramatic writer, maybe even a cinematic writer. So here I was, outside of Paris with nothing to do. What did God want? I have learned that this following Scripture is true, as is all Scripture, but when it resounds in your life and becomes Rhema, and not just Logos, one knows that one knows that one knows that God makes all things work together for our good, even when we don't understand the plan.

And we know that all things work together for good to those who love God, to those who are the called according to His purpose (Romans 8:28)*.*

Upon arriving in the suburbs of Paris, I joined a prayer group. In this group there happened to be one of the most amazing English-speaking, French women I had ever met. She had a doctorate in English literature, her spoken English was impeccable, and she liked reading my books. I had already published four novels in English: *Sleeping With Demons*, *Wild Card*, *Wild Fire*, and *Buried Lies*. Timidly, I asked her to translate *Buried Lies*. To my sheer delight, she agreed. She gave up her life for this translation, since she still worked ten to twelve hours a day, and whatever spare time she had before was now spent on my translation.

I lived with a couple who ran a word-of-mouth bed and breakfast, and they rented one of their bedrooms to me full time. When I discovered that they were publishers of Christian books, I was dumbfounded. They published *Buried Lies* as *Mensonges Enfouis* in French! The path of God is

KNOWING GOD AS OUR DADDY

best looked at over the shoulder, because in no way could I have planned all this in advance!

The studio, which now was deprived of my radio stories, also published books, and we negotiated that I would write twelve books, about 100 pages each, in a series called "The Destined Series." Each book would present one subject in the Bible: Success, Healing, Love, Faith, Grace, Joy, in Christ, in the Spirit, Battle Ready, New Life, to Heal, and To Know God Personally.

A longtime friend offered to work for me, she's a digital genius! For the website, my friend Jennifer Cunha, who first self-published my short stories in three volumes in English, now manages the site. There are seven "pages" on the site, three of which I continually write for: "Opening the Bible," which has two sub-pages: "Bible Studies" and "Bible Snacks." "Opening the Heart," which has two sub-pages: "Effective Prayer" and "Naked Before God." "Opening the Mind," which has two sub-pages: "Intimacy Personified" (web-stories) and "Who Am I?" The site is dual languages, French and English, just a click changes the language. My books are available for purchase on the page *Store*. How did I go from a radio ministry to all this? God has taken care of all the details up until now, so I'm expecting the same, if not better quality that He has always given.

I miss doing the radio programs, but I must admit, my books and other written works reach far more people as a book just keeps on going, whereas a radio program is aired once and then it's done for. Writing is my way of serving God, and like everything God does, what we do for Him, fulfils the desires of our hearts. Writing makes me happier than anything else I do with my life. That's destiny: the very basic ingredient that makes each one of us tick, the desires of our hearts, the profound satisfaction that makes us sing with the angels and sleep in the arms of God.

Somebody called me a nomad and it hurt my feelings. They said God called me that. So, when alone I challenged Him, why would He use such a derogatory term to describe me? He interrupted and said, "A nomad is somebody who is searching for something." Suddenly, I realized that I have been searching for something for thirty-three years.

As I mentioned before, when I was first born again, I wanted to learn as fast as I could, so I went to every meeting being held in the Bay Area. One night, I attended a service, and during the awesome Praise and Worship (with my arms raised overhead, tears streaming down my cheeks), I heard myself say, "I'll go to Grass Valley." And then I stopped and asked myself, "What is Grass Valley?"

The next night, I was in another church on the opposite side of the city, and during the awesome Praise and Worship (with my arms raised and tears streaming down my cheeks), I suddenly had a vision. My first. It just dropped into me. I saw a building built into a hillside. The shape of the building was that of a cross, but a cross I had never seen. With the edges of the roof lined with white lights, from the air one could definitely tell it was a cross. The part built into the hillside housed a theatre seating 1,500 people. There was a two-story coffee shop/bookstore, plus a restaurant, dozens of individual prayer rooms, auditoriums for teaching, a chapel and beautiful grounds surrounding it. The vision was so clear, even now, thirty-three years later, I can vividly remember each detail.

KNOWING GOD AS OUR DADDY

In northern California between San Francisco and the Sierra Mountains, there is a town called Grass Valley. Of course, I drove up there. I didn't know a soul, and nothing of any consequence happened while I strolled around town, praying. I knew of a church in a nearby valley whose offices were on Grass Valley Road, so I wrote up the vision and offered to come explain it to them, *as it obviously must be for them.*

They replied that women do not receive visions, and no, I would not be welcome, but if my husband wanted to bring the vision to their next men's breakfast, they could discuss it. So, we did that. But they decided it was not for them. I didn't know what to do with a vision, so I let it sit on the back burner—so to speak. However, when I arrived in France and put my foot on French soil, I heard the voice of the Lord say, "This is My Grass Valley. Everything grows here. This is where I want that building planted." I believed God. He hasn't told me when or where, but I believe in the right time He will cause that building to be built, and it will be the place where Christian arts will be developed and presented to the world. Arts are the gifting of God, which He gave to the French. By the way, the only place I found a cross with the same shape as the building, is in France. It's a Huguenot cross.

I've tried to get out of France, but I know now this country is my destiny. One time when I was back in the States, I went to a huge meeting of 50,000 people in Dallas, Texas. The speaker was making a plea for people to go as missionaries to South America. I raised my hands to heaven and said, "Lord, I'll go. Send me." Suddenly, I saw His face in front of mine. He said, "Marty, I said France." I felt like such a failure in France, I crumpled and said, "Oh, Lord, I'm so unworthy." I dropped my head, and suddenly I saw Satan's face in front of mine, so I abruptly pulled my head back up. Again, the face of Jesus was in front of me. Again, He said, "Marty, I said France." Again, I crumpled, put my face down and instantly saw the face of Satan, so I jerked my head back up. Again Jesus, in front of my face, said, "Marty, I said France." And I did not let my face fall again. I am called there.

While praying not too long ago, I suddenly was back in the vision on the day I wore a white bridal gown into the throne room. Once again, I sat on God's left knee, and I leaned my head on His left shoulder. This time He wore a crown with five prongs sticking out. One of the prongs pierced my head, but I didn't feel it; I just knew it.

"Now," He said, "we can reason together." He imparted more wisdom about the subjects He had whispered to me in that previous experience. I saw myself lecturing one of my granddaughters to stop dreaming about having a husband, a home, and children. I told her to seek God, and these things would come to her.

The Lord said, "Shouldn't you follow your own advice?"

I realized I put too much importance on the Center being built, whereas I, too, need to first seek the Lord. He responded to my thoughts, "I'd like for you to concentrate on your writing." For some reason, I had a file-card pad in my hand on which, years ago, I had written a prosperity Scripture on each card, as that Center will cost a big bundle, and I wanted to work on my faith for finances before I needed the money to build! At the back of the pad I had written the prosperity I would receive, and the dates it would happen. Horrified

KNOWING GOD AS OUR DADDY

at my immaturity, I ripped those cards out and destroyed them. I repented. We can ask for dates on which He is going to do things, and He may or may not tell us, but we aren't allowed to order God to do things on the dates we choose for something to happen! The Lord said, "Keep writing. That will make The Center happen." These days my nose is in my computer, writing. My next step is to write a Christian series for television. He is the one father who truly does know best!

To know God as Father means we will know Him as our divine Daddy. Certain pastors, when talking about their father, call him *Daddy*. "Well, Daddy said . . ." I like that. I like knowing that as a mature adult I can still know Him as Daddy. Knowing God as Father also causes us to know ourselves and to know our destiny. He has it all planned and written up in a book. "The Book of Marty" written by God. There's also one written about you. Knowing God as Father will introduce us to the supernatural Kingdom of God, which is what Jesus said He came to preach. It will establish order and make the entire Body of Christ work as it should. Knowing God as our Father will prepare us for the eternity we will spend with Him. And right now, it's time to sit on His knee and have a long talk. It's time to know Him better.

Chapter Three

KNOWING GOD AS JESUS CHRIST

The church I attended as a child was a wonderful place. Many kids my age attended, so I had numerous friends, and the adults organized really fun times for everybody. My mother taught the adult Sunday school. She didn't teach about Jesus because she didn't know Him. I'm hopeful that on her deathbed she received Him. I didn't learn about Him in my children's Sunday school either. Yes, we learned His stories, and we learned lots of nice ways to behave; we were a humanitarian group, but Jesus and His salvation? No. Nothing. Not at home, not at church. Thank God I found Him in a parking lot!

Knowing our Heavenly Father is one thing, actually the most important thing, because we will spend eternity with Him, but the path begins by knowing Jesus. He is the part of God who came to earth to draw each one of us into the Kingdom of Heaven, and to preserve us for our eternity with our Father. With His Blood He paid the price to absolve our sins, destroy them completely, thereby purifying us. We were lost, and Jesus came as the light in the darkness that drew us out of our caves where we were hiding, and into the safety of His sheepfold. During that trip, we became born again and surrendered our lives to Jesus Christ and designated Him as our Lord and Savior.

Every trip taken is different from all others as each of us is a unique creation of God, a prodigal son or daughter who made wrong choices, and now who must humble ourselves. When we do, God will hike up His robes and come running to embrace us and wrap us in the finest robes. Jesus takes us on that road back home.

As an adult, I found church to be like a big cocktail party, but without the alcohol. Everyone circulated, everyone chatted; however, on such a superficial level I wondered why anyone came. My attendance diminished bit by bit, especially since I married a Catholic who never went to church, and the prospect of spreading the fat Sunday San Francisco Chronicle on the table and reading it with a big pot of coffee nearby became more and more appealing.

Church stopped for me on one of the last shopping days before Christmas when I laid down on the back pew of a Catholic Church. The night before, after the children were asleep, I fussed with the Christmas decorations while my husband sat on the couch, listening to Christmas carols. I stopped in front of him and asked a question. When he answered, my life began its final descent into hell on earth.

I asked, "What's wrong with our marriage?

Normally, when I asked that question, he replied, "Nothing." But this time he said, "I like boys."

That response registered a blank in my head. With all the brilliance I could muster I asked, "What?"

"I like men."

KNOWING GOD AS JESUS CHRIST

Still stumped I questioned, "What does that mean?"

"I like having sex with men! Okay!? Is that clear enough for you!?"

I don't know what happened next, all I know is that I found myself on my back on the floor with his hands pinning my shoulders down. It took me a minute to register what he was saying as he repeatedly said, "Don't hate me. Don't hate me."

Hate him? I had no knowledge of hating him. What I did feel, overwhelmingly, was that he hated me. He hated me because I'm a woman. (I found out later he was the female partner of his homosexual couple.) That's what was wrong with our marriage. I didn't know whether to laugh or cry. I asked who his lover was and he told me; a man I knew well, a man he worked with. They had been lovers when I first met my husband and through all the preparations for our big, fancy wedding. They had been lovers after our honeymoon, in fact, right up until this very moment, ten years into our marriage, and after the birth of two children, they had been, still were, and wanted to continue being lovers.

I don't remember sleeping that night. I roamed the house. He slept quite soundly. The next day I left the kids with him while I went for a walk, and that's when the tears started. We lived close to Fisherman's Wharf, so I wandered there and mingled with the last-minute Christmas shoppers. My tears were copious, and I just didn't care when people looked at me in a shocked or disapproving way. They didn't have my problem. How could they know what this deceit felt like?

I needed an answer to a very basic question, one that any person asks in any given situation. "What shall I do?" I had no idea how to answer that question, nor did I know of anyone who could give me an answer. Did I know anyone who had ever faced this situation before? No. No one.

After a couple of hours of walking, talking to myself, walking, and floundering, I started home. Suddenly, the picture of a Catholic church stood out in my mind. I'd never been inside this particular church, but it was near my house, so I went there. It was empty, cavernous, somber, even dusky inside. I was still crying when I lay down on the back pew. I think a priest came and peeked at me, but then he tip-toed away; however, when I left, he was kneeling at the railing up front. I'm sure he was praying for me.

As I poured my woes out to the echoing church, I saw something; at least I think I saw something. It was as if a dove had been sitting in the rafters and it flew down to me. It said, "Stay with him" and then it disappeared into the duskiness. The tears stopped, I regrouped my forces, sat up, noticed the priest at the altar rail, and I rushed out of the church.

What does one do without divine help? What does one do when they have children to raise, a house to keep, and a life to manage? I did the only thing that I probably knew to do—I entered a deep depression. It was a slow decline, but it ended with me being unable to even get dressed, or to clean house. I sat in my rocking chair for three months and planned my death. But then my wonderful, God-given children came home from school, climbed into my lap, wiped away my tears, and together we made dinner. They probably saved my life because I knew I couldn't commit suicide and leave them parentless.

In such a depression one has no energy to say "No" to absolutely unwanted invitations. So, when my aunt invited me to a prayer meeting, I said okay, I'd go. I was visiting her

KNOWING GOD AS JESUS CHRIST

in the foothills of northern California where the temperature is moderate in the summers, but on this occasion, the evening was extraordinarily hot. Her church had pulled chairs into the parking lot and made a circle for the prayer group.

As I sat down, I realized I had never done this before. I had never talked to Jesus, and I realized I was willing to do so, now. When I closed my eyes, I immediately saw a huge ball of fire and light, right in the middle of the circle. The fire was so hot I felt it would burn my skin. A wind blew so strongly I felt it pushed my hair back. My logical mind always has to explain things, and it said, "Oh, the sun is just setting and is on you full force, and a wind has come up." I opened one eye and the sun had already set and there wasn't even a breeze in the trees. I closed my eye again and the phenomenon was still there. As I watched, the classic form of Jesus—the image on the walls of my childhood church—stepped out of the light, held His arms out, and said, "Come to Me."

It was so real that I was in the process of getting out of my chair when the Pastor said, "Amen." Then I was obligated to open my eyes, and the phenomenon disappeared, but something surrounded me and in fact went home with me that night. The something spoke day and night, telling me how much I was loved, telling me about the hope God had for my life, and telling me how important I was. It encouraged me to attend church, and I chose the Episcopalian Church next door to the Catholic Church where I lay in the pew.

I chose that one for all the wrong reasons; I know that now. It had been built by a renowned architect and was absolutely beautiful. A children's choir wore adorable gowns, and both my children sang well and were quickly accepted into that choir. But that *something* that lived with me now, chose that church for the right reason. Every time I entered the door to the sanctuary, I would cry. Embarrassed, I sat under an eave where no one else would sit. I never went forward for communion, I never stopped for coffee in the courtyard, and the parishioners left me to myself.

One Sunday morning on the way to church, I heard an audible voice. It said, "Marty, you have come a long way, but you have one more step to take."

Shocked to hear a disembodied voice I simply reacted, "What?"

The voice said, "You must say with your mouth that I am your Lord."

Rage rose up inside me because no one was going to be my Lord except ME! I didn't cry when I entered the sanctuary that morning; I must have glowed with anger. But I knew, somehow, I just knew, that if I said no to this something with me who wanted to be my Lord, I would lose that something, and I didn't want that. It was making me feel too good about myself. Better than I had ever felt in my entire life.

For the first time, I went forward for communion, and as chance would have it—if there really is something called chance—I was alone, kneeling at the altar rail. I looked up at the cross and said, "Okay, Jesus. You are my Lord."

Something cold and nasty left my body by the bottom of my feet and something warm and wonderful entered my chest coming directly from the cross. At that precise moment a gentleman I did not know came with the cup of wine and said, "Marty, the blood of Jesus shed for you."

KNOWING GOD AS JESUS CHRIST

After church, in the courtyard where I had stopped for coffee, he apologized to me. He said he had argued with the Lord that he should not use the name Marty because it was a man's name, and he would offend me if he said that, but the Lord insisted. I assured him he did the right thing. I was born again. Jesus had come for me, and I, fortunately, had the good sense to surrender my life to Him.

Furthermore, this lovely Episcopal Church was heavily involved in something called *Cursillo*. Originated by a Catholic priest in Spain, it was designed for all denominations to participate, but only the Episcopalians would join with the Catholics. It was life-changing. Several of the ladies wanted to sponsor me in taking the four-day weekend, however, *Cursillo* required that husbands take it first on the men's weekend, and then the wife could take the women's weekend. My husband agreed to go.

He said on the Saturday night, after two days of heart-wrenching testimonies and talks given by ordinary men about how Jesus changed their lives, the *Cursillistas* went into the sanctuary where a large wooden cross lay on the steps to the altar. Each man was given a very small piece of paper and were asked to write his sins on it. My husband couldn't see how all of his sins would fit, but he wrote some things. Then they gave each man a hammer and a nail and asked them to go nail their sins on the cross. He did that. All the men returned to their seats. Then they were asked if they wanted to surrender to Jesus and serve Him for the rest of their lives, would they again come to the cross and receive a miniature cross to wear around their necks.

My husband debated with himself whether or not to go forward, when he felt a hand on his shoulder, and he heard someone whisper in his ear, "Why not?"

He said to himself, "Why not?" and so he stood, but when he looked behind him, there was no one who could have put his hand on his shoulder and whispered in his ear. That's when my husband's tears started, and they didn't stop for about a week. He wore that cross day and night.

Of course, the mark of success of that weekend at *Cursillo*, for me, would have been if the lover had been removed from my husband's life. But that didn't happen. It made him love the man more. Now he was free to express what he had been feeling all these years. Fortunately for me, I fell so deeply in love with Jesus that my husband's histrionics had no effect on me, and I would in no way allow my children to be a part of a homosexual household.

During my *Cursillo*, I heard the word "charismatic" and it was as if my heart had split in two. I didn't know what it meant; I just knew I had to have it. Afterwards, I stumbled across an ad in the *San Francisco Chronicle* inviting the public to a Catholic Charismatic Mass, and my husband and I went. I'd never seen anything like it, nor even heard about it. People sang with their hands raised all the way up in the air, tears streaming down their faces—in a church service—and the most beautiful a cappella singing I had ever heard with words from some strange language.

I found a brochure on the pew about another Catholic Church in Berkley giving a Charismatic weekend for those who wanted this Baptism of the Holy Spirit. We went to that as well, and I was gloriously submerged into the Holy Spirit and spoke with tongues of men and angels. Who baptized

KNOWING GOD AS JESUS CHRIST

me like that? Jesus Christ. He gave me this wonderful gift that now put me in a position to understand biblical mysteries, to talk to God directly in a language only He could understand, and I could be given the interpretation of what I said. I discovered that Jesus needs the Holy Spirit to speak through His people like that because He can do nothing on the earth unless it is spoken out by man.

The next summer, my aunt invited my children and me to attend a Charismatic Family Camp with her. My husband couldn't take the time off work to go. The very first night in camp, my children were in their groups, and I sat in the sanctuary, listening to the Chairman of the camp explain the week to come. The Holy Spirit said to me, "You will be up there doing that."

I immediately reacted, "There is no way I could do that!" Fear of public speaking is greater than the fear of death!

Every night after that I heard the same thing, "You will be up there doing that."

My reaction was always the same, "No way!" At the end of the week I was asked to join the council to plan next year's camp. I accepted. And yes, I did become Chairman for two glorious years before moving away to attend Bible School. I learned so much about working with the Holy Spirit from being Chairman that I can't begin to express my growth. I just need to say, I am grateful for that opportunity.

In these early years, I was so hungry for God that I got out of bed every morning at 5:00 a.m. and spent two hours in prayer. Then I woke the kids up and got them off to school. After that, I spent two hours reading the Bible. I did have a job, but my boss liked me so much, he allowed me to work my own hours, so my Christianity didn't get in the way of my outer life.

One day in prayer, I heard the words, "Go to Rhema." I knew the word *Rhema* meant "the word of God," so I figured the Lord wanted me to read the Bible more. Dutifully, I added another half hour to my Bible reading, until a friend dropped by to say the Lord sent her to tell me to go to Rhema.

I said, "Well, then, what is Rhema?" She told me it was a Bible school in Tulsa, Oklahoma. I'd never heard of a thing called a Bible school, much less of one in Tulsa, Oklahoma. But I found the address, wrote to them, filled in the application, as did my husband (he was sick and tired of running our restaurants and wanted to sell them), and I sent them off. We were accepted. But I needed a confirmation. I needed to know this was really God.

My husband and I went away for a weekend, and therefore visited a church we didn't know. For some reason, I expected to receive our confirmation during this church service. Nothing happened until the Pastor's closing prayer. He began to stutter and finally said, "Oh, Lord, let Your Rhema settle in their hearts." Well! That was enough confirmation for me! We put the restaurants up for sale, rented out our house, and moved our family to Tulsa, Oklahoma.

Because I had spent so much time in prayer, I thought I was a hot shot pray-er, but when I stepped into the school's Prayer School, I found out what a novice I was. These people were somewhere in the heavenlies with their prayers, somewhere I had never been. I said, "Oh, Lord, I want that! Take me there!" Every afternoon when I joined the other 300 people in Prayer School, I prayed with urgency, and one day, suddenly, I was there.

KNOWING GOD AS JESUS CHRIST

I saw a pair of shoes, quite distinct, walking through a field of grain. I knew they were my feet, and that I was carrying the Gospel. I asked, "Where is that?" He elongated the vision to show me the map of France, and I said, "Oh, no, not there!" I had been to France one time, to Paris only, and I found the people to be rude, crude, and unrefined, and I thought if I never go back, it will be too soon! Now the Lord was sending me to this once detestable place.

Three years later, we moved to France—all four of us—and I was there by obedience only. But one day as I walked down the street headed for the bakery, love for the French dropped into my spirit like a ton of feathers. Since that day, I have loved the French, and they have loved me.

However, after three years, we came back to the States in order to divorce. Just like every other country, France has evil spirits that want to rule and reign. One of them is sexual deviation. My husband had given up his lover years before, but in France, under such weighty oppression, he fell back into his old ways. I couldn't take any more. However, once at home, I couldn't bring myself to divorce. I did not want to be single.

I finally confessed all to the wife of the head of the ministry we belonged to. She arranged for us to have an appointment with a very powerful prayer group in Minnesota. I'd heard about this group, but I didn't have the connections to obtain an appointment. She did. We had to wait three months, and one week before our trip to Minnesota, the leader of the prayer group called and said that my husband could not enter the prayer room. He did not want to be set free. I asked how she knew this, and she said the Lord told her. We believed her to be misinformed, and we both went for the appointment.

However, they would not let him in the door. They said if he came in that would prevent the Lord from doing anything for me. I wondered why they wanted to pray for me, but I wasn't going to waste the trip, so I went in the prayer room, and my husband went back to the hotel.

In the cocoon of that prayer group, praying quietly behind me, I encountered the most sickening demon I had ever seen—and by this time I had seen some—he had one arm wrapped tightly around my head, telling me what to think. His other arm, wrapped tightly around my husband's chest, told him what to feel. I commanded that demon to leave me, and I watched his arm around my head fall to the floor and disintegrate, however, the arm around his chest carried him away. I understood that he must now leave my life, or that demon controlling his emotions would bring in more friends, and my life would be even more miserable.

After a month, my husband moved into a facility run by the Assemblies of God where they take men with sexual addictions, house them, and get them set free. It took three years, but he finally became free of all homosexuality. He stayed there, as a member of the staff, and successfully helped hundreds of men be free of everything from pornography, adultery, rape, homosexuality, pedophilia, etc.

Once my husband enrolled in the program, I waited a few months for results. When no good news came, the Lord told me to get a divorce and return to France. It was the best thing I had ever done for my husband, as it made him take responsibility for his life. Before I left, the director of the facility told me they had never run into such a hard heart toward God as my husband had. Five weeks after the divorce, I was back in France, and I believe the Lord has told me I will

KNOWING GOD AS JESUS CHRIST

finish my life and my work right there. I'm expecting God to do a mighty work in France, and I'm thrilled to be able to participate in His Great Pentecost! I believe He is rebuilding His Church right there on the land that was once called the Daughter of the Catholic Church.

Since my new birth, Church has taken on a whole new meaning. Church is where Jesus calls His people to gather for staff meetings. We don't operate like an earthly staff because we're heavenly, divine staff.

> [9] *And they sang a new song, saying: "You are worthy to take the scroll, And to open its seals; For You were slain, And have redeemed us to God by Your blood Out of every tribe and tongue and people and nation,*
>
> [10] *And have made us kings and priests to our God; And we shall reign on the earth."* (Revelation 5:9, 10).

We're all on His staff, we all have destinies to fulfill, and we are all a vital part of His Body. Not one of us can be discarded as worthless. Each of us has tremendous worth! The day I realized that church was more than a cocktail party was the day I decided to embrace Jesus as my husband.

I suddenly saw it. I saw that God builds His church by revelation, and on this day, I had a revelation that God had extruded Himself into three parts: Himself being the Father, the Creator, the Power, and the Authority. Jesus became the head of the Church, the director of all God's people—and their accomplishments—for His glory. And the Holy Spirit became the best friend of each new-born Christian, living on the inside of them to guide them and teach them, to console them, and encourage them.

I also saw that if Jesus was the director of the staff meeting, then I'd better embrace Him. I told Him I didn't know how to accept a husband, but that I wanted Him to be mine, and I went into His outstretched arms. They'd been waiting for me ever since I saw Him in that big ball of light.

I had a terrible time getting to know Jesus because He was supposed to be my husband, and whereas I embraced God as my Daddy because I never had one, I did have a husband. My earthly husband did not set any kind of an example of heavenly husbandry, so I came to Jesus with suspicion and hesitancy. But when I put aside that earthly example, I discovered that Jesus is the Personification of God. He is every bit God, exactly like His Father, as much like His Father as His Father is like Him. He's made of the same stuff. He is all love. That doesn't mean He cannot be stern. With sceptics, He is stern. With evil, He is ferocious. With His own, He is love; He is God.

Jesus said to him, "Have I been with you so long, and yet you have not known Me, Philip? He who has seen Me has seen the Father; so how can you say, 'Show us the Father' (John 14:9)?

God is open for us to ask Him anything we want to know. When I wanted to know about the trinity, He said that He and Jesus and the Holy Spirit are three different expressions of the same person. They all have the same character, the same mind, the same sensibilities, but each one has different functions. When Jesus came to the earth, He became a person and exhibited who God is. He is Perfect Everything.

KNOWING GOD AS JESUS CHRIST

Jesus is Love Personified. After He and I became close, I had trouble with a woman who wanted me out of her church. Every Sunday she spread a new rumor about me, and they were not spoken with Christian kindness. My presence grieved her. The Lord told me to flood her with love and kindness, and He coached me how to do it.

Whatever she said about me that was negative, I said the same thing about her in the positive. If she said, "Oh, Marty's so self-centered! She just wants all the attention on herself." I said, "Oh, that sweet woman is so selfless. She is always giving, giving, giving." She had the church on her side because she was the Pastor's wife. She lived in a wheel-chair, her body inundated with Muscular Dystrophy. I prayed for her, and she walked out of her wheelchair. No one can contend for someone's healing without completely loving the person they're praying for. Otherwise, the prayer has no substance. The love I demonstrated toward her won the day, and she became my champion in that church.

Jesus is Truth Personified. He is the Word of God, that's true, and He is also willing to tell the truth with such love that it doesn't hurt anybody's feelings. The first time I asked Him if there was anything about me that displeased Him, He answered immediately. I would have preferred that He would need to consider whether or not there was something displeasing, but noooo, He had an answer ready. He said, "You spend too much time with my enemy." (And no, I didn't purposely just sit at the enemy's doorstep waiting for a dinner invitation.) I knew right away what He meant. I spent too much time worrying and wondering how things were going to work. Both of those are definitely sins because I belong to

Him 100%. In His care there is no room for worry, nor does He need my help in planning my life.

I don't know about other Christians, but He doesn't let me get by with telling half-truths. A half-truth makes *me* look good, and the *other person* look bad. In fact, it is a lie because only the whole truth is the truth. He makes me go back to the people I've lied to and confess my error. He also doesn't let me pretend I love someone when I haven't forgiven them. Holding something against someone leaves no room for love.

The first week I spent at the family Charismatic Christian Camp, I learned how to live many principles of Christ. One night, He woke me up and told me to take my notebook and pen. I had a flashlight, so I didn't disturb the others in my cabin. When notebook and pen were poised, He instructed me to write down the names of everyone I needed to forgive. I thought it would be an easy list, as I could think of five people right away; I wrote their names. But then another name popped up, and as I wrote another name appeared. This continued all night! By morning I had over 1,000 names in my notebook and writer's cramp.

Then He asked me to forgive each one. I thought I had to go find them and forgive them, but He said no, that it was for my benefit that I needed to forgive, so that I wouldn't carry any burdens. He also told me it was not my job to restore these people, it was His, and I was to leave them in His hands until He finished the job. I started with the first name on my list, naturally it was that of my husband. I said, "I forgive my husband." Then I sat back and realized it wasn't true. I said it again. Still no interior change. Then I remembered a Scripture I had read.

KNOWING GOD AS JESUS CHRIST

"A good man out of the good treasure of his heart brings forth good; and an evil man out of the evil treasure of his heart brings forth evil. For out of the abundance of the heart his mouth speaks" (Luke 6:45).

Obviously, I was going to have to change my heart to agree with the words I spoke from my mouth. Not knowing what else to do, I repeated over and over and over, "I forgive my husband." Finally, a breaking came, my emotions boiled over, I cried, and then I knew I had forgiven him. The passion inside and the words spoken into the spiritual kingdom around us, must coincide for the two worlds to converge. After that My husband's derision for me and his repulsion of me no longer mattered. They were not my problem, they were his.

Jesus is Intimacy Personified. The Catholic Church in Berkley where I became submerged in the Holy Spirit, held Friday night healing services. I didn't need healing, but the anointing was so strong that it compelled me to attend. After watching the proceedings for several months, I decided it was my turn to go up front and ask for prayer. The priest of this parish was the softest, kindest, most intelligent, most forthright man of the cloth I had ever met, even up to this day. He trained over forty people in the protocol of prayer, mostly women made up the membership in his teams of three, and I was directed to a prayer team.

The woman in charge asked what I wanted from the Lord. I said, in all sincerity, "Ask Him to forgive me for being the awful person that I am." She immediately placed a hand on my shoulder and started praying in tongues.

Disgusted, she stuttered to a stop. "I can't pray a prayer like that! He loves you just the way you are. You go home, read Song of Solomon because it is a love letter written to you, and allow Him to love you."

I went home, put on my pajamas, took my Bible, and climbed into bed. With the first words of that book my tears fell, and they did not quit. No one could love me like that. I had never experienced such passion for me, sullied, insignificant me. Not from my family, not from anyone. I determined I would read Song of Solomon every night until I could read it without crying, then I put my Bible aside and turned out the light.

Curled up in fetal position, I heard someone whispering to me. "Let Me rock you to sleep." I could actually feel His arms encircling me, and we laid there, spoon fashion, as we gently swayed. I don't know if I actually moved or not, but it certainly felt like I did. This happened every night for three months until the tears stopped and something deep inside me was satisfied. He continues to be tenderly intimate with me; sometimes when I'm reading, I'll sense His arm resting across my shoulders as He peers at the Bible with me. He's been known to take my arm as I'm crossing a street.

Now that I'm alone, there are certain things that could be difficult for me, were it not for His Presence. For instance, I had an itch in the middle of my upper back that I just could not reach with enough force to satisfy that itch. I asked, "Jesus? Would you scratch my back for me, please?" And He did. From the inside!

I like going to restaurants and normally women don't do that alone. But I'm not the kind that stays at home because of social restriction, so I invite Jesus to go out to eat with me.

KNOWING GOD AS JESUS CHRIST

I've learned to let Him choose the restaurant, as His choice is always more expensive than I would choose. The first time this happened, I complained, "I can't afford that one."

He replied, "Who said you were paying the bill?" So we went, had a lovely time, and when it came time to pay the bill, my only choice was to pull out my credit card. However, within a few days an amount of money arrived in my mailbox, unexpected money that more than paid for the meal. It always works like that.

In the restaurant, I sit in one seat, and Jesus sits across from me, and if I were to talk to Him out loud, I would be quickly escorted from the restaurant because I'm pretty sure no one can see Him but me. So, I bring a notebook and a pen. I write what I want to say to Him. Then I push those two items across the table. When He is finished speaking, I pull them back and write what He had to say to me. You may think I'm crazy, but I learn more about Him in this casual, intimate, way, than any other avenue I have for our relationship. I try to make Friday night our date night, but it doesn't always work out that way.

Another intimate moment with the Lord happened because of my "Bucket List." I don't actually have one, but I was telling the Lord that before I died, I would really like to ski again. I loved snow-skiing. I never had good form, but I'd take on any slope and either make it down the hill on my skis or on my back, and I would be enthralled with the ride. When I told Him this, I figured the best I could do would be a little cross-country skiing.

He asked, "Why do you think you can only do things here?" Then He took me on a tour of a part of heaven I had never seen before. When one analyses heaven from what the

Bible has to say, the capital city, The New Jerusalem, covers an area the size of one half the United States. That's just a city. He showed me the mountains where I will be able to ski to my heart's content. It would take a man walking three months to cross those ski slopes, and that was just one ski area! The Lord and I then put on skis and skied like champions. Jumping off a ski jump? Well, I've now done it! I can hardly wait to get there!

Jesus is God's Will Personified. In the beginning when I was learning how to walk and talk with the Lord, I had a lot of internal chaos, and as a result could not function as a normal adult. I tried everything the church had to offer—deliverance, emotional healing, ridding myself of generational curses, etc. All such programs worked for a while, but eventually the condition would return. Finally, I turned to the Lord, as He was the only one who could help me.

He said it was not the bad things that happened to me that ruined my life—illegitimate birth, raped by my stepfather for nine years, the value of my talents desecrated, marrying a homosexual, etc. It was what I thought about myself because of what happened to me that ruined me. The lies that I believed became my truth and rendered me ineffective in every domain. He gave me a prayer process to identify the lie, observe how that lie had twisted my life, receive the truth, and have the Lord rip out the lie, and plant the truth.

I used that prayer process on more than two hundred lies over a period of twenty-five years. Then one day, the Lord said it was time to write a book about the prayer process to introduce it to the world. I wrote "Buried Lies." People started reading the book and asked me to produce a workshop in which I would lead them through the prayer process.

KNOWING GOD AS JESUS CHRIST

I thought this sounded wise, as the first time I did it, I spent seven hours struggling through the prayer, because we are not accustomed to praying so deeply, nor to obtaining the answer before we quit the prayer. Then they asked that I write a workbook so that they could continue doing the prayer process at home. I wrote "Uprooting Buried Lies."

It is God's Will that we be free from the devil's purposes in order to live an abundant life with the Lord. Every time I lead one of those workshops, I am so grateful I am allowed to help other people be set free. Nothing is more exciting than to see them drop the shackles of bondage and walk free knowing the truth.

For instance, the first lie I uncovered was, "I don't have the right to be here." Because I thought this was the truth, I tried to hide myself wherever I went. But when I learned the truth, which was, "There are no unwanted children in My Kingdom," I realized my importance to God, and I found freedom. The second lie was, "My only value is to be used for sex." And when I discovered my truth about this, "My value is in the Lord Jesus Christ who lives in me," it changed the way I perceived myself. The third lie was, "I am too stupid to be successful." But the truth that replaced this lie brought incredible joy to my life. The truth the Lord showed me was, "I created you to write." It was His idea, not mine. It's not my intelligence that counts, it's His! There is absolutely nothing I like doing more than writing with Him.

Jesus is the Perfect Everything, and that includes being the Perfect Husband and the Perfect God. He supplies all my needs. He pays for everything. He treats me to things I really enjoy. He chooses my clothing in the mornings. He insists that I talk everything over with Him. He likes spending quality time with me alone. If I lose something, He finds it for me. I lost one of my favorite earrings one time; couldn't find it anywhere. When I woke up the next morning it was sitting on the lid of the closed jewelry box! He thanks me for what I do for Him. He tells me how wonderful He thinks I am.

Jesus is my Lord, my King, my God!

Chapter Four

KNOWING GOD AS THE HOLY SPIRIT

The Holy Spirit is God. He is the Spirit of God; God's inseparable part. And yet, He was sent to us, and He is the one who seals us so that we are forever attached to Him.

> THE MOMENT WE BELIEVE IN THE GOSPEL, THE MOMENT WE RECEIVE JESUS AS LORD, THE MOMENT WE ARE PLUNGED INTO CHRIST IN THE TRUE BAPTISM, THE HOLY SPIRIT SEALS US THERE. HALLELUJAH!

In Him you also trusted, after you heard the word of truth, the gospel of your salvation; in whom also, having believed, you were sealed with the Holy Spirit of promise, (Ephesians 1:13).

One day, while in the process of writing about the Love of God, I realized I had no good illustrations from my own life to share. I went to the Lord and asked Him to show me how much He loves me so that I could write about it. That afternoon, being a fine, warm time in the fall, I walked to the supermarket instead of driving. I wore my wallet dangling from a strap over my shoulder. When I arrived at the supermarket, there was no strap dangling from my shoulder, and hence, no wallet. Everything pertinent to my life was in that billfold!

I could have panicked, but I didn't, I could have hyperventilated, but I made myself sit down, and then I prayed. The Lord told me I would find my wallet on the sidewalk. I hurried through the pains of searching the sidewalk from the supermarket to where I started. Suddenly, a young woman I didn't know said, "Marty? Marty Delmon?" In all honesty I thought this was someone who had seen my picture on the back of one of my books and wanted to stop and talk about it for a while, whereas I was screaming inside, "I don't have time for this!"

She said, "We just turned your wallet over to the police. I'll have my husband call them and ask them to come back and give it to you. We found it on the sidewalk right over there." Both the police and this young couple went through my billfold with a fine-tooth comb, yet nothing was missing when they handed it back to me. I tried twice to give the couple a reward, I only had 45 Euros in my billfold, but they wouldn't take it. I became very suspicious of the Lord.

"Did You arrange this? Was this an example of how much You love me?"

He said, "Marty, you have no idea how much I protect you during the day. Yes, this was an example of My love for you. The devil would like to get you away from serving Me, in fact, he would like to kill you, but My mighty hand is over you, and he cannot even get close." I needed no further examples of His love for me. That mighty hand is the Holy

KNOWING GOD AS THE HOLY SPIRIT

Spirit who does the work on the earth. Look at what He does for us!

> THE HOLY SPIRIT IS HERE TO GUIDE ME INTO EVERYTHING THE FATHER WANTS FOR ME AND EVERYTHING JESUS MY LORD HAS PREPARED FOR ME.

"However, when He, the Spirit of truth, has come, He will guide you into all truth; for He will not speak on His own authority, but whatever He hears He will speak; and He will tell you things to come" (John 16:13).

> IF I'LL LET THE HOLY SPIRIT PRAY THROUGH ME, THEN THE PLANS AND PURPOSES OF MY FATHER AND MY LORD CAN BE IMPRINTED ON THIS KINGDOM OF THE EARTH, AND I WILL WALK OUT MY PERFECT DESTINY.

And they were all filled with the Holy Spirit and began to speak with other tongues, as the Spirit gave them utterance (Acts 2:4).

Likewise, the Spirit also helps in our weaknesses. For we do not know what we should pray for as we ought, but the Spirit Himself makes intercession for us with groanings which cannot be uttered (Romans 8:26).

> IF I INSIST ON MY OWN WAY, THE HOLY SPIRIT WILL LET ME HAVE IT, BUT IF I WILL SURRENDER TO THE WILL OF GOD, IT WILL BE DONE IN MY LIFE.

¹¹ No one knows the things of God except the Spirit of God.

¹² Now we have received, not the spirit of the world, but the Spirit who is from God, that we might know the things that have been freely given to us by God.

¹³ These things we also speak, not in words which man's wisdom teaches but which the Holy Spirit teaches, comparing spiritual things with spiritual.

¹⁴ But the natural man does not receive the things of the Spirit of God, for they are foolishness to him; nor can he know them, because they are spiritually discerned (1 Corinthians 2:11–14).

THE HOLY SPIRIT IS WITH ME 24/7.

If we live in the Spirit, let us also walk in the Spirit (Galatians 5:25).

By this we know that we abide in Him, and He in us, because He has given us of His Spirit (1 John 4:13).

"The Spirit of truth, whom the world cannot receive, because it neither sees Him nor knows Him; but you know Him, for He dwells with you and will be in you" (John 14:17).

HE WON'T DO ANYTHING I DON'T WANT HIM TO DO. IF I DON'T EMPLOY HIS SERVICES, THEN HE PATIENTLY WAITS UNTIL I TIRE OF TRYING TO MAKE THINGS WORK BY MYSELF, AND I CALL ON HIM. HE IS HERE TO BE MY HELPER.

KNOWING GOD AS THE HOLY SPIRIT

"But when the Helper comes, whom I shall send to you from the Father, the Spirit of truth who proceeds from the Father, He will testify of Me" (John 15:26).

⁷ "Nevertheless, I tell you the truth. It is to your advantage that I go away; for if I do not go away, the Helper will not come to you; but if I depart, I will send Him to you.

⁸ And when He has come, He will convict the world of sin, and of righteousness, and of judgment" (John 16:7, 8).

GOD NEVER GOES BACK ON HIS WORD.

He told the Israelites they would have whatever they said. They whined, "We're all going to die in the desert." And they did. God tells the angels to do whatever we say as long as our words agree with His Word.

"It is the Spirit who gives life; the flesh profits nothing. The words that I speak to you are spirit, and they are life" (John 6:63).

"For the Holy Spirit will teach you in that very hour what you ought to say" (Luke 12:12).

OF THE THREE IN THE TRINITY—THE FATHER, JESUS, AND THE HOLY SPIRIT—I BELIEVE THE HOLY SPIRIT HAS THE HARDEST JOB. THANK GOODNESS HE CARRIES THE POWER AND SHARES IT WITH ME!

"But you shall receive power when the Holy Spirit has come upon you; and you shall be witnesses to Me in Jerusalem, and in all Judea and Samaria, and to the end of the earth" (Acts 1:8).

Now may the God of hope fill you with all joy and peace in believing, that you may abound in hope by the power of the Holy Spirit (Romans 15:13).

HE IS HERE TO TEACH ME.

He is here to teach each one of the seven billion people on this earth, as well. His Spirit still covers the earth and dips down to enter whatever soul invites Him to live inside; in other words, He is huge and can do all things, at all times, in all places. No matter where we start from, whether we have no knowledge of what Jesus has accomplished for us, or if we have a massive amount of cultural understanding of Christianity, the Holy Spirit is going to take us from where we are to where Jesus wants us to be.

"But the Helper, the Holy Spirit, whom the Father will send in My name, He will teach you all things, and bring to your remembrance all things that I said to you" (John 14:26).

Clearly you are an epistle of Christ, ministered by us, written not with ink but by the Spirit of the living God, not on tablets of stone but on tablets of flesh, that is, of the heart (2 Corinthians 3:3).

KNOWING GOD AS THE HOLY SPIRIT

THE HOLY SPIRIT DISPERSES POWER GIFTS, ALLOWING ME TO HAVE THE PRIVILEGE OF ACTUALLY WORKING WITH GOD.

[4] There are diversities of gifts, but the same Spirit.

[7] But the manifestation of the Spirit is given to each one for the profit of all:

[8] for to one is given the word of wisdom through the Spirit, to another the word of knowledge through the same Spirit,

[9] to another faith by the same Spirit, to another gifts of healings by the same Spirit,

[11] But one and the same Spirit works all these things, distributing to each one individually as He wills (1 Corinthians 12:4, 7–9, 11).

THE HOLY SPIRIT IS THE ONE WHO SUBMERGED ME INTO THE BODY OF JESUS CHRIST, AND AS I ENTERED THAT BODY, I DRANK THE HOLY SPIRIT INTO MY BODY TO LIVE THERE TO GUIDE, TEACH, AND HELP ME. HE IS THE ONE WHO CHANGES ME INTO THE IMAGE OF MY LORD.

For by one Spirit we were all baptized into one body--whether Jews or Greeks, whether slaves or free--and have all been made to drink into one Spirit (1 Corinthians 12:13).

[17] Now the Lord is the Spirit; and where the Spirit of the Lord is, there is liberty.

¹⁸ *But we all, with unveiled face, beholding as in a mirror the glory of the Lord, are being transformed into the same image from glory to glory, just as by the Spirit of the Lord* (2 Corinthians 3:17, 18).

> IF I'M GOING TO BE LIKE JESUS, THEN MY INNER PROPULSION AND MY OUTER BEHAVIOR MUST REFLECT HIM. I MUST BEAR HIS FRUIT.

²² *But the fruit of the Spirit is love, joy, peace, longsuffering, kindness, goodness, faithfulness,*

²³ *gentleness, self-control. Against such there is no law* (Galatians 5:22, 23).

> OUR GOD IS PERFECT EVERYTHING. HE IS PERFECT FATHER. HE IS PERFECT HEAD OF THE CHURCH. HE IS PERFECT HELPER. HE WAITS ON US TO THROW OUR HANDS UP IN THE AIR IN PERFECT SURRENDER. HE WANTS US TO BE HIS PERFECT FRIEND.

Why not?

Made in the USA
Monee, IL
09 February 2021